JUST A MINUTE MEDITATIONS

Finding Inner Peace

BY KATHRYN J. HERMES, FSP

Pauline
BOOKS & MEDIA
Boston

ISBN 10: 0-8198-1693-0
ISBN 13: 978-0-8198-1693-1

Library of Congress Control Number: 2023939076

Portions of this book have been excerpted and adapted from *Cherished by the Lord* (Pauline Books & Media, 2012).

Cover design by Tisa Muico

Published by Pauline Books & Media, 50 Saint Pauls Avenue, Boston, MA 02130-3491

Printed in the USA

www.pauline.org

Pauline Books & Media is the publishing house of the Daughters of St. Paul, an international congregation of women religious serving the Church with the communications media.

1 2 3 4 5 6 7 8 9 30 29 28 27 26 25 24

Contents

Introduction

Has anyone ever smiled at you so radiantly that you felt they were saying, "I'm delighted you are here"? At least once in a lifetime we each should receive that gift! When someone says to us that he or she is glad we exist, our heart leaps and we feel at home. Because we rarely receive the message that such a smile brings, we suffer. We conclude that no one really wants us as a friend or considers us of value. Life's anxieties, trials, and tragedies threaten to rob us of our inner peace and to drown us in darkness.

God has smiled upon us since the creation of the world. These meditations are a simple support to help you lift your eyes to the face of the One who loves you more than you could ever imagine. As you pray with them day after day, may you discover how God wants you to be content, as content as a baby in its mother's arms. Each meditation is carefully chosen to amaze you with what God has done for you in his gracious and marvelous act of redemption.

Here is an easy method of reading these meditations that I use. It will unlock in your heart the courage to believe in God's desire to save and bless you in all things:

1. God will lead you to be interested in certain meditations. Go wherever God leads you. You don't have to read these in order unless you'd like to.
2. Before you read, remember a moment when someone delighted in having you around. Tell God how grateful you are for that gift of love.
3. Begin to read the meditation. Relish what you read. Notice which words and phrases seem to light a fire that warms your heart. Enjoy the safety and beauty of that moment.
4. Talk to God about what is burdening you right now. Then reread the words of Scripture in the meditation, hearing them as if God were speaking to you by name. Even place your name right in the passage and imagine God speaking these words to you directly. Notice what it is like and tell God how grateful you are.

My desire for you is that you will bask in God's gaze as it rests upon you, that you will find calm and quiet for your soul, and that you will be content as a small child to sleep in his care for you.

1

My Love Shall Never Fail You

O afflicted one, storm-battered and unconsoled,
  I lay your pavements in carnelians,
  your foundations in sapphires;
I will make your battlements of rubies,
  your gates of jewels,
  and all your walls of precious stones.
Though the mountains fall away
  and the hills be shaken,
My love shall never fall away from you
  nor my covenant of peace be shaken.

ISAIAH 54:11–12, 10 (NABRE)

I truly appreciate the way Isaiah offers assurances to his people of God's love for them. This is a promise made to a people who had been defeated and exiled by the Babylonians. The promise, "O afflicted one, storm-battered and unconsoled . . . my love shall never fall away," speaks directly to the hearts of the exiles longing for home.

I invite you to hear these words whispered straight to your own heart in moments of anxiety. Those of us who find our lives in a relentless cycle of anxious worry about challenging or unjust situations often find it difficult to tolerate uncertainty. Even though we mentally try to assure ourselves of all the possibilities we have to help ourselves, our hearts are still racing. Remember, there is one thing, and only one thing, that is irrevocably certain. God loves you. God is more powerful than whatever negative situation could threaten you. And God keeps his promises. With his covenant of love, he assures you of the fullness of his blessing and protection from harm.

When the storms batter my life, O Lord, console me. Be faithful to your promises.

2

Do Not Be Troubled

> "Do not let your hearts be troubled. Believe in God, believe also in me." Thomas said to him, "Lord, we do not know where you are going. How can we know the way?" Jesus said to him, "I am the way, and the truth, and the life."
>
> JOHN 14:1, 5–6

It is shortly before Jesus is arrested. He has just announced to the apostles that he will be with them only a little longer. There must have been a high level of anxiety in the room as the followers of Jesus tried to understand what was happening. Jesus doesn't enter the whirlpool of their fears. He tells them to believe. When a person is filled with anxious concern, it seems almost cruel to say, "Do not let your hearts be troubled." Nevertheless, those are the very words of Jesus. He is affirming that indeed we do have a choice. We can acknowledge our anxiety, take a deep breath, and ask

Jesus to help us to walk through the difficult situation with faith in him. We may still feel overwhelmed with fear, but the very fear will become our teacher.

Thomas worriedly reminds Jesus, "We don't know where you are going." Anxiety tries to convince us that if we can just figure it all out we'll find peace of heart. Jesus, however, says to Thomas that this is not about getting it right. It is about trusting that Jesus himself is the one who will lead us rightly to what is true and to the ultimate end for which we are created. "I am the way, the truth, and the life."

Jesus, Way, Truth, and Life, I trust in you.

3

A New Name

> Then Abram fell on his face; and God said to him, "As for me, this is my covenant with you: You shall be the ancestor of a multitude of nations. No longer shall your name be Abram, but your name shall be Abraham. . . . I will establish my covenant between me and you, and your offspring after you throughout their generations, for an everlasting covenant, to be God to you and to your offspring after you."
>
> GENESIS 17:3–5, 7

I often imagine what this pivotal religious experience must have been like for Abraham: he, the creature, before God the Creator. By entering into the covenant that God was offering him, Abraham was facing the unknown. He was being called out of his comfort zone. God makes a covenant also with us. In this covenant we discover what it means to be truly human: sought out by God, loved, embraced, committed to by the One who was, who is, and who ever will be. This everlasting covenant God makes with us assures us that the true identity we so desperately seek is found in the arms of a loving God who will never abandon us.

My Lord, I hunger so much to know my life has meaning. Is it too much to ask you to call me by a new name? Guide me to discover who you've created me to be.

4
An Extraordinary Mercy

Sing to the Lord a new song,
  his praise in the assembly of the faithful.
For the Lord takes delight in his people,
  honors the poor with victory.

Psalm 149:1, 4 (NABRE)

God loves us as if we were the center of his universe! We who have died and risen with Christ, we in whom the Son abides, we for whom Jesus answered to his Father with his life and with his death—we are the object of God's delight. We are chosen by God. Jesus spent his thirty-three years of life serving our needs with his own hands, wiping up our mess with his own blood, opening our future with his own death. God makes the impossible possible; the unbelievable reality. What is unlovable will melt in his hands. What is ostentatious will thrill to be a cascade of lilies in a blooming field, clothed only with the brilliance God gives them. What is afraid will stand with the certainty of the resurrection. We shy away from grandeur and expectations, but we are drawn with confidence by this extraordinary mercy that will delight us eternally.

O Love! You see my anxieties and my longing for inner tranquility! Give me eyes to see your extraordinary mercy at work in my life.

5

A Future of Hope

> For I know well the plans I have in mind for you—oracle of the LORD—plans for your welfare and not for woe, so as to give you a future of hope. When you call me, and come and pray to me, I will listen to you.
>
> JEREMIAH 29:11–12 (NABRE)

When someone else has the plan, I relax. I am grateful when I can be part of the process without having to lead the parade. I feel this way particularly when I place my life in the hands of God, trusting in his providential plan for my life.

When I forget that the plans the Lord has for me are for my welfare, it is usually because I'm mentally tangled in recalling, reliving, and rehearsing. I see the future with hope, instead, when I talk to God about what's happening. I speak with the Lord simply, just like I'd talk to a dear friend. "This just happened, Lord. Do you see it? There is no use in me occupying myself with it any further. I know there are things I still need to say and do about this situation. I know that you will provide for everything at the proper time. At the right moment I know you will inspire the thought or lead me to the action that will bring about your plans. For the rest, I let it be."

O God, fill my spirit with your peace. I know you have plans for my well-being and so I cast all my cares on you.

6
You Are Not Alone

> Therefore, since we are surrounded by so great a cloud of witnesses, let us rid ourselves of every burden and sin that clings to us and persevere in running the race that lies before us while keeping our eyes fixed on Jesus.
>
> Hebrews 12:1–2 (NABRE)

The author of Hebrews is writing to a Christian community that has lost property and been persecuted for their belief in Jesus. Negative life experiences had led to weariness, and they were doubting their commitment to Jesus. Whether or not we personally have lived through persecution, we are living in a time of deep uneasiness about the state of the world and of the economy. Violence breaks out on our streets and in our schools. We live in a culture marked by painful losses and skyrocketing anxiety and depression.

These words in Hebrews are written for you and me. We are not alone. Even if we feel lonely or there is no one to help us, we are always surrounded by the saints. At every moment we can call on them for assistance. They have run the race ahead of us and lived through similar struggles. Remember: You are not alone!

So when anxiety and worry fill your mind with a hundred what-ifs, take your eyes off the future and fix them on Jesus. Panic keeps us in a whirlpool centered on our own losses. Instead, keep your eyes on Jesus. Talk to him. Listen to him. Reach out to the community of disciples right here on this earth, and together persevere like the saints before us in running the race.

Jesus, keep my eyes fixed ever on your face.

7

I Will Show You How to Face Your Fear

> Then Jesus came with them to a place called Gethsemane, and he said to his disciples, "Sit here while I go over there and pray." He advanced a little and fell prostrate in prayer, saying, "My Father, if it is possible, let this cup pass from me; yet, not as I will, but as you will."
>
> MATTHEW 26:36, 39 (NABRE)

Jesus spoke directly to his Father about what he was most afraid of that night in the Garden of Olives, the night before he died. Jesus didn't let his anguish obscure his trust in his Father. Our anguish when we are faced with something truly stressful can be so strong that we believe all the thoughts running through our heads. "I can't do this." "I'm no good." "I knew everything would end like this." "Things will never change." "This proves that God isn't good."

Jesus shows us how to face anguish and anxiety. He knelt in his sorrow and agony. He talked directly to his Father about all he was experiencing. Finally, he had so great a trust in his Father's love for him that he could say, "Not my will but yours be done." Ultimately the Father didn't save Jesus from crucifixion and death, but through his passion and death Jesus destroyed death's power. He defeated it by dying himself and then rising as Victor over death. He conquered what we most deeply fear in order to deliver all those who, through fear or death, were subject to lifelong slavery—you and me.

Father, I trust you to care for me.

8

Keep Your Eyes Open

> Let love be genuine; hate what is evil, hold fast to what is good; love one another with mutual affection; outdo one another in showing honor. Do not lag in zeal, be ardent in spirit, serve the Lord. Rejoice in hope, be patient in suffering, persevere in prayer.
>
> ROMANS 12:9–12

In autumn, the colorful array of changing leaves turns into winter's barren bleakness, symbolizing what often happens to our spirits. We live a spiritual rhythm of ups and downs, fullness and barrenness, blossom and decay. The downs pave the way for the ups; barrenness creates the possibility of refilling; times of decay fertilize the new blossoms in our lives.

When Saint Paul says, "Be ardent in spirit," he is no doubt referring to this ongoing cycle of life and death. But I believe he is thinking of something more. I once came across this definition of prayer: "To pray is to think of Jesus while loving him." It was as if a fire had been kindled within me. Those simple words ignited an ardent fire in my brittle spirit that burned away bad habits and replaced them with a yearning for holiness. It is the Holy Spirit who ignites these spiritual fires that make us long for more. Paul knew this, because the Spirit had transformed his ways of thinking, acting, and loving, making him a new creature in Christ. So keep your eyes open. The Spirit will use something in your everyday experience to ignite your spirit and inflame your heart.

Holy Spirit, stir up the ashes of my life and relight my inner fire. Amen.

9

Undeserved Blessings

> "For the kingdom of heaven is like a landowner who went out early in the morning to hire laborers for his vineyard. After agreeing with the laborers for the usual daily wage, he sent them into his vineyard. . . . When those hired about five o'clock came, each of them received the usual daily wage. Now when the first came, they thought they would receive more; but each of them also received the usual daily wage. And when they received it, they grumbled against the landowner. . . . But he replied to one of them, 'Friend, I am doing you no wrong; did you not agree with me for the usual daily wage? . . . Or are you envious because I am generous?'"
>
> MATTHEW 20:1–2, 9–11, 13, 15

In your Christian life, what do you consider your "daily wage"? This parable strikes to the heart of being Christian in today's culture of entitlement. We are owed nothing. It is rather a privilege that we know the

Commandments and have experienced the joy of being and doing for others in the spirit of Christ. In this parable, the grumbling workers miss the point entirely. Their attitude is, "God owes me." Jesus was teaching them to realize instead, "God loves me." In the ecstasy of that love they need do nothing but rejoice that others are given a share in it, even if they have done little or nothing to deserve it.

Jesus, this message is hard: to rejoice when others are blessed undeservedly. Help me know that I have been blessed undeservedly. Change my heart!

10

His Gracious Act of Redemption

O LORD, my heart is not lifted up,
  my eyes are not raised too high;
I do not occupy myself with things
  too great and too marvelous for me.
But I have calmed and quieted my soul,
  like a weaned child with its mother;
  my soul is like the weaned child that is with me.
O Israel, hope in the LORD
  from this time on and forevermore.

PSALM 131

A contented child in its mother's arms feels safe. Contentment also means being completely satisfied, with no need to look for anything else. A quiet child isn't squirming to get out of its mother's hold to go running off. As adults, however, contentment doesn't come so easily. We no longer experience personal, financial, or even national security. Each new release of a digital gadget restarts the itch of wanting more things until we have decided whether or not to purchase it. Many of us don't particularly like the role that is ours in the world: it might be too small, too tight, too hectic, too heavy. We cast around for something else that seems like a better fit. Psalm 131 offers us a secret for contentment: look to God and not to yourself. See what God has done in his gracious and marvelous act of redemption. Renounce any source of significance or security other than God.

O God, help me to quiet my soul, and to be content with all you give me, asleep in your care for me.

11

We're Beloved, Desired, Died For

> "To the Lord our God belongs justice; to us, people of Judah and inhabitants of Jerusalem, to be shamefaced, as on this day—to us, our kings, rulers, priests, and prophets, and our ancestors. We have sinned in the LORD'S sight and disobeyed him. We have not listened to the voice of the LORD, our God, so as to follow the precepts the LORD set before us."
>
> BARUCH 1:15–18 (NABRE)

It has been said that if the Song of Songs were the only book of Scripture, we would have all we need to understand God and salvation history. The conjugal imagery of the lover's desire for the beloved in this short, unpretentious book of love poems unlocks the meaning of the rest of the Bible, and of this passage from Baruch in particular. Why are we "shamefaced"? Why does Jesus mourn over us as he did over the cities that had witnessed his miracles and power? Because we have been beloved, courted, desired, died for. We have clung to pennies when God wanted to make us millionaires. The impassioned divine Lover would have us be the darling of his heart. This passage is not an angry invective, but the words of broken hearts—both human and divine. These hearts that desire love will not rest until they are loved and have proven their love to each other.

What can I do to prove my love for you, O everlasting Love?

12

When Anxiety Is Intertwined with Guilt

For as the heavens are high above the earth,
so great is his steadfast love toward those who fear him;
as far as the east is from the west,
so far he removes our transgressions from us.
As a father has compassion for his children,
so the LORD has compassion for those who fear him.
For he knows how we were made;
he remembers that we are dust.

PSALM 103:11–14

There are times when anxiety seems to take over my life. I think it happens to most people at least some of the time, but to others of us it can absorb a lot of our attention and energy. However, when anxiety is intertwined with guilt, it is especially debilitating.

A friend told me once how he couldn't bring himself to receive the Eucharist because he felt so guilty. The guilt was so intense that he was almost crippled by anxiety. My friend, who suffers from scrupulosity and OCD, was almost crushed under this burden of anxiety that arose from a sense of right and wrong gone askew. When we suffer with anxiety, we can forget that God tells us again and again that he understands that we are dust, that we are fragile, and that we are so in need of him.

Know that when God looks at you, he sees not how you don't measure up, but how beautiful you are as the work of his hands and his dear child.

Lord, I rest in your compassion for me.

13

Wordlessly Embrace His Feet

After the sabbath, as the first day of the week was dawning, Mary Magdalene and the other Mary came to see the tomb. . . . The angel said . . . "Then go quickly and tell his disciples, 'He has been raised from the dead, and he is going before you to Galilee; there you will see him.'" . . . Then they went away quickly from the tomb, fearful yet overjoyed, and ran to announce this to his disciples. And behold, Jesus met them on their way and greeted them. They approached, embraced his feet, and did him homage. Then Jesus said to them, "Do not be afraid. Go tell my brothers to go to Galilee, and there they will see me."

MATTHEW 28:1, 5, 7–10 (NABRE)

Jesus' death had shattered the world of his first followers. I can imagine the news of the crucifixion passing quickly from one disciple to another: the hushed suspense, the quiet agony, the shock, the fear, the sorrow. Then suddenly, less than three days later, they literally run into him, alive. Jesus must have stood there before the women with exquisite tenderness, his heart full of compassion for their sorrow. I wonder if they stopped to notice the kindness in his eyes. The events that seem to lead us to Calvary, and the power of our fears, are not greater than the love of our Savior. Jesus stands before you also with great kindness in his eyes and tenderness in his heart, reminding you again and again: I am alive!

You are alive! You are here! Do not let my fears keep me from seeing you!

14

An Ongoing Conversation

O that you would tear open the heavens and come down,
  so that the mountains would quake at your presence. . . .
When you did awesome deeds that we did not expect,
  you came down, the mountains quaked at your presence. . . .
Yet, O LORD, you are our Father;
  we are the clay, and you are our potter;
  we are all the work of your hand.

ISAIAH 64:1, 3, 8

One of my favorite images of God is that of a potter. Once, my mother took us kids to a ceramics class. It was okay, but as soon as we finished, my interest dropped. I wasn't invested. God, however, is deeply invested in what he creates. While some commentators see the image of potter as one of power—God chooses how to shape the clay—for me the image of potter is an image of love. I can imagine God listening closely to everything we say as we experience him shaping our lives. The shaping of the vessel is part of an ongoing conversation of love between potter and clay. On a particularly busy day, I (the clay) may tell God (the potter) that I am tired. I need help. God delights to bend over the little vessel he is loving into being and to care for me.

Listen closely, God, to the whisper of my heart. Bend over your creature, here, and let me know your ever-tender love.

15

Courageous Creativity

When he was in Bethany reclining at table in the house of Simon the leper, a woman came with an alabaster jar of perfumed oil, costly genuine spikenard. She broke the alabaster jar and poured it on his head. There were some who were indignant. "Why has there been this waste of perfumed oil? It could have been sold for more than three hundred days' wages and the money given to the poor." They were infuriated with her. Jesus said, "Let her alone. Why do you make trouble for her? She has done a good thing for me."

Mark 14:3–6 (NABRE)

The broken alabaster jar is a courageous act of great creativity. This unnamed woman must have been a contemplative person. She had space and margins in her life. She cultivated a restful spirit. Silence and solitude allowed her heart to find peace.

At this dinner, shortly before Judas would betray the Master, when everyone was affected by the growing clouds of danger gathering around Jesus, this woman caught Jesus' attention with an extravagant and creative action. Out of her broken jar she poured an amount of precious spikenard that would have cost someone's annual salary at the time. The broken bottle symbolizes that she didn't want to hold back anything for herself. Jesus understood the meaning of the gesture, for he himself would hold back nothing for himself, offering his life for our salvation. This passage from Mark teaches us that even in times of overwhelm and anxiety, we can offer others hope when we look for spaces of rest and creativity.

Do not hold back from me, Lord! Do not let me hold back from you!

16

Beautiful Lives

> They watched him to see whether he would cure him on the sabbath, so that they might accuse him. And he said to the man who had the withered hand, "Come forward." Then he said to them, "Is it lawful to do good or to do harm on the sabbath, to save life or to kill?" But they were silent. He looked around at them with anger; he was grieved at their hardness of heart and said to the man, "Stretch out your hand." He stretched it out, and his hand was restored.
>
> MARK 3:2–5

This Gospel reading is about broken hearts. Jesus was grieved, saddened, heartbroken at the Pharisees' hardness of heart. The saints know that when we shut God out of our lives, not only are our hearts broken, but so also is God's. The saints thirsted for the opportunity to be with God in the same way a person in love desires to please his or her loved one. Whatever their age or vocation, every aspect of their day was filled with Jesus.

They gave God their voice to speak his words, their hands and feet to serve others, their eyes to reflect God's love and care to all whom they met.

On the physical level, clogged arteries can lead to heart attacks and death. On the spiritual level, we may need to unblock our spiritual arteries. Let us arouse our love, stoke the fires of devotion, read the word of God, and receive God's grace in the sacraments to keep our hearts soft and open to the gift of God.

Lord, set my heart on fire!

17

I Need You

> "Two men went up to the temple to pray, one a Pharisee and the other a tax collector. The Pharisee, standing by himself, was praying thus, 'God, I thank you that I am not like other people: thieves, rogues, adulterers, or even like this tax collector. I fast twice a week; I give a tenth of all my income.' But the tax collector, standing far off, would not even look up to heaven, but was beating his breast and saying, 'God, be merciful to me, a sinner!' I tell you, this man went down to his home justified rather than the other; for all who exalt themselves will be humbled, but all who humble themselves will be exalted."
>
> LUKE 18:10–14

Luke's parables are stories that help us understand what Jesus means in the Beatitudes when he declares fortunate those whose only recourse is God. We see the widow who cries out for legal justice, and the children who in their simplicity cry out for blessing. The blind man at Jericho cries out for his one great need: to see God. And in this selection, we have the tax collector who mourns his sins and cries out for forgiveness. Only the Pharisee, a good man and a strict observer of the Law, is not fortunate. He saw no need to reach out of himself and beg God for justice, blessing, mercy, or vision. The Pharisee felt he had everything he wanted or needed. Jesus, instead, came for those who had no one but God to depend on. Do you need God? If you do, you are indeed fortunate.

I need you, my God. Accept my heart reaching out to you.

18
Feelings of Insecurity Frighten Me

> The women played and sang:
>
> "Saul has slain his thousands,
> David his tens of thousands."
>
> Saul was very angry and resentful of the song, for he thought: "They give David tens of thousands, but only thousands to me. All that remains for him is the kingship." From that day on, Saul kept a jealous eye on David.
>
> 1 SAMUEL 18:7–9 (NABRE)

Sometimes just a word that highlights how someone else is better than we are can make our insecurity flare up. Especially when we are holding on to something that makes us feel good about ourselves, we can become very touchy and anxious when it is threatened. Basically all of us who travel together on this precarious journey we call life suffer from at least a mild case of insecurity. Once in a while we are reminded that what we hang on to for security could be taken away from us.

We discover that the people we think we live in solidarity with are actually a threat. Both Saul and David were insecure. Both were holding on to the admiration of the crowds. Jonathan, King Saul's son, was a levelheaded peacemaker because he wasn't holding on to anything. He was looking out for the good of both Saul and David. Neither his father nor his friend was a threat to him.

Jesus, feelings of insecurity frighten me. I don't like to feel anxious or jealous. When I feel threatened, send me a Jonathan. Amen.

19

We Are Powerless

> After [Jesus] had finished speaking, he said to Simon, "Put out into deep water and lower your nets for a catch." Simon said in reply, "Master, we have worked hard all night and have caught nothing, but at your command I will lower the nets." When they had done this, they caught a great number of fish and their nets were tearing. . . . When Simon Peter saw this, he fell at the knees of Jesus and said, "Depart from me, Lord, for I am a sinful man."
>
> LUKE 5:4–6, 8 (NABRE)

Poor Peter! He's just been overwhelmed by God's magnificent generosity. Suddenly Peter realizes who is in his boat. When we witness a remarkable display of God's presence and love, our first reaction is often to create distance. I think that's because such experiences make it clear to us on a very deep level that we are not as powerful as we think. Like Peter—the professional fisherman who couldn't force the fish into his net but discovered that someone else could fill his nets on command—we realize our smallness in the midst of a creation so vast it can't be controlled or explained. We are indeed powerless in the face of so many things in life. Jesus wants to work miracles for you, in your boat, where you live and work today—miracles that will help you see what he wants to do in your life and the mission he has given you. Stay awake!

Come, Jesus, into my boat. I long to be surprised by your generosity today. I long to witness the evidence of your care for me. Come!

20

Love Always Triumphs

Thus says the LORD:
I am going to restore the fortunes of the tents of Jacob,
  and have compassion on his dwellings. . . .
Their prince shall be one of their own,
  their ruler shall come from their midst;
I will bring him near, and he shall approach me,
  for who would otherwise dare to approach me?
    says the LORD.
And you shall be my people,
  and I will be your God.

JEREMIAH 30:18, 21–22

Here the Lord makes an astonishing commitment of love! It's astonishing because it is not promised to people who have proven themselves worthy of such recognition from God. Rather, Jeremiah had clearly stated that the people's sin was so grievous that their wound was incurable. They had no hope for healing, no relief in sight for their pain. Such cruel words could only come from a broken heart. Often Scripture portrays God as brokenhearted at the disloyalty of his people. He abandons them to their own devices and exile. But love, even when betrayed, still triumphs. "I am going to restore the fortunes of the tents of Jacob. . . ." No matter what we've done, no matter how awful the circumstances of our lives, which could even cause us to cry out against God, love will triumph. God will not let us go. We are his people and he is our God.

Do not let me go, my God. Hold on to me even when I would run away. Let your love conquer me! I claim you as my God, for you have claimed me as your child.

21
The Reason I'm Still Alive

The LORD is my shepherd, I shall not want.
Even though I walk through the darkest valley,
    I fear no evil;
for you are with me;
    your rod and your staff—
    they comfort me.
Surely goodness and mercy shall follow me
    all the days of my life,
and I shall dwell in the house of the LORD
    my whole life long.

PSALM 23:1, 4, 6

I speak often with Sarah, whose husband turned her and their two girls out of their home in order to marry another woman. Sarah spent almost a year in homeless shelters with her children. Gradually she earned enough money to move to another town, to find new schools for the girls, and eventually to buy a small house. Psalm 23 is one of her favorite psalms: The Lord is my shepherd. . . . He leads me, he restores my soul, he gives me courage, he anoints me, and I shall live with him forever. The psalmist declares unshakable faith in the love of God even in the darkest valley. I am moved when Sarah tells me how much God loves her. She knows it is only God who has helped her survive all she has been through: "He is the reason I am still alive." From the psalmist and from Sarah, I've learned that adoration, trust in God, and self-abandonment are the truly Christian response to the vicissitudes of our life journey.

Thank you, Lord, for all those who witness to your fidelity as they walk through dark valleys. They are a gift to me.

22

Touching God's Presence

The angel said to her, "Do not be afraid, Mary, for you have found favor with God. And now, you will conceive in your womb and bear a son, and you will name him Jesus. He will be great, and will be called the Son of the Most High, and the Lord God will give to him the throne of his ancestor David. He will reign over the house of Jacob forever, and of his kingdom there will be no end."

LUKE 1:30–33

A woman once said to me, "You seem to be able to touch God's presence as if it were real." AS IF it were real! Without realizing it, she had put into words our modern anguish that God seems so remote. He seems to be nothing more than invisible gas—a ghostly non-reality, a deity without the face or voice we long to see and hear. This modern conception of God is far from the triune God, the Father whose Son became Mary's baby—personal, compassionate, involved, committed to us. This Gospel passage speaks of messages from God, commitments of faith, obedient adoration: things that can easily be brushed off as the uninformed piety of the simpleminded. After all, science and technology claim to know what really makes the world go round. This Gospel, however, puts us squarely in the realm of the reality that only faith can see. God is as real and involved in our lives as when he asked Mary to be the mother of his Son.

Mary, show us God's face once more. Teach us to hear his voice again and again. Amen.

23

A Tidal Wave of Love

When they had crucified him, they divided his clothes among themselves by casting lots; then they sat down there and kept watch over him. . . . From noon on, darkness came over the whole land until three in the afternoon. And about three o'clock Jesus cried with a loud voice. . . . "My God, my God, why have you forsaken me?" . . . Then Jesus cried again with a loud voice and breathed his last.

MATTHEW 27:35–36, 45–46, 50

Crucified and forsaken on the cross, Jesus shows us to what great extent we are called to love. We cannot see the Persons of the Trinity in their relationships with one another. But we can see how Jesus, the Incarnate Son of God, has loved us. Jesus came and carried all the weight of our burden. He took upon himself not only our sin, but our death, our experience of frustrated relationships, our alienation, our forsakenness.

He did not love us from afar. He nursed us back to health with the healing balm of his death and paid the price of our salvation with his own blood. What would happen if we loved one another this way? It is hard, I must admit. Efficiency, the bottom line, advantage, and personal plans have to give way and crumble before the onslaught of this tidal wave of love. But, oh, how much more blessed and fulfilled would our lives be? And the world? Would it not be a much more beautiful place to live?

Lord, I resolve to live a life of total, self-forgetful gift. May my love contribute to peace in the world.

24

Build Up the Body of Christ

> For just as the body is one and has many members, and all the members of the body, though many, are one body, so it is with Christ. For in the one Spirit we were all baptized into one body—Jews or Greeks, slaves or free—and we were all made to drink of one Spirit. . . .
>
> Now you are the body of Christ and individually members of it.
>
> 1 CORINTHIANS 12:12–13, 27

Together we are Christ in the world. Together. Each of us is not simply a cell in the body of Christ. Each of us, individually and together, is Christ's body. This means that whenever one of us is present to another, Christ is present. When someone ministers to us, Christ is ministering. When I teach someone, Christ is teaching. We do not need to be afraid of conflicts. They are created by our struggles to grow in maturity and to overcome individualism, collectivism, isolation, and self-serving agendas. These conflicts sand away the sharp edges of our characters and transform our selfishness until the body can live together as one, in harmony, in mutual obedience, growing in love and freedom. Each of us can build up the body of Christ within ourselves, for the sake of others, in the Church and in service to the world.

How can it be that I—and each of us—have been raised to the honor of being members of the body of Christ? For this, Lord, I praise you.

25

Where to Look for Jesus

While they were talking and discussing, Jesus himself came near and went with them, but their eyes were kept from recognizing him. . . . Then he said to them, "Oh, how foolish you are, and how slow of heart to believe all that the prophets have declared!" Then beginning with Moses and all the prophets, he interpreted to them the things about himself in all the scriptures. . . .

When he was at the table with them, he took bread, blessed and broke it, and gave it to them. Then their eyes were opened, and they recognized him.

LUKE 24:15–16, 25, 27, 30–31

Luke's account of the two disciples on the road to Emmaus teaches me three lessons about finding Jesus. First, on my own, like the two disciples, the best I can do is attempt to figure things out. Jesus meets me on the road I am walking. He will reveal to me a different way of seeing things: the way of faith. Second, Jesus tells me not to be afraid of the crises I or others experience. They will all, like the crucifixion, one day be mysteriously taken up and transfigured in a manner none of us can know right now. Third, we will find Jesus always, whenever we need him, in the breaking of the bread. Jesus left us the Eucharist so that he would be here with us always and we would be able to find him. And all this comes to us through the Church.

Jesus, our Life, come to meet us. When we are anxious or discouraged, come alongside us. Draw us to the Eucharist.

26

See with the Eyes of the Heart

> "Then the king will say to those on his right, 'Come, you who are blessed by my Father. Inherit the kingdom prepared for you from the foundation of the world. For I was hungry and you gave me food, I was thirsty and you gave me drink, a stranger and you welcomed me, naked and you clothed me, ill and you cared for me, in prison and you visited me.' . . . And the king will say to them in reply, 'Amen, I say to you, whatever you did for one of these least brothers of mine, you did for me.'"
>
> MATTHEW 25:34–36, 40 (NABRE)

Each of us, and all of us together, share the world's resources for the period of time that is our life. And yet the world is at a seemingly impossible impasse, as Jesus said: the poor you will always have with you (see Matthew 26:11). What can break that impasse open? The prayer of the rich and the prayer of the poor, the love of the rich and the love of the poor. When people can see with the eyes of the heart, they will see Christ in each other. People, whether rich or poor, will become the secret makers of a new history that will hasten the coming of the kingdom of God. Jesus gives us the key: whatever we do to others, we do to him.

May I join hands and hearts with all the people I encounter. May I think about them with compassion, speak to them with gentleness, and shoulder with them the responsibility of shaping a new way for humanity.

27

God Is Bursting into the World

> Then Jesus called the twelve together and gave them power and authority over all demons and to cure diseases, and he sent them out to proclaim the kingdom of God and to heal. He said to them, "Take nothing for your journey, no staff, nor bag, nor bread, nor money—not even an extra tunic. Whatever house you enter, stay there, and leave from there."
>
> LUKE 9:1–4

Jesus sent the apostles to proclaim the kingdom of God—an announcement that God is bursting into the world in the person of Jesus Christ. With this vision of reality, we become grounded in our truest self: we are citizens of God's kingdom. Without this vision of reality, every stress, obstacle, or cause of dismay we encounter can knock us off course. Faith is the light and power that nourishes our thoughts and builds true self-esteem. It gives us the confidence to believe in God's sustaining love for us.

I don't know about you, but it is so easy for me to read about faith yet still find that my thoughts get lost in every anxiety and distortion, leading me far away from the joy of living in the kingdom of God. I shrink before the onslaught of disturbing news, fearing that negativity and not love may be the center of the universe. My thoughts can trap me and tear me away from what alone can heal me: the good news that God is here.

Jesus, steady my mind, that I may look into each situation with the security of knowing myself a child of the Father, at home in your kingdom. Amen.

28

You Still Have a Role to Play

> Moses was tending the flock of his father-in-law Jethro, the priest of Midian. Leading the flock beyond the wilderness, he came to the mountain of God, Horeb. There the angel of the LORD appeared to him as fire flaming out of a bush. When he looked, although the bush was on fire, it was not being consumed. When the LORD saw that he had turned aside to look, God called out to him from the bush: Moses! Moses! He answered, "Here I am."
>
> But the LORD said: Now, go! I am sending you to Pharaoh to bring my people, the Israelites, out of Egypt.
>
> EXODUS 3:1–4, 7, 10 (NABRE)

At one point in his life, Moses had everything going for him. His mother's care had preserved his life when other newborn Hebrew boys had been killed by Pharaoh's decree. Moses was raised in Pharaoh's palace, and presumably he would have had possibilities other Hebrews couldn't access. However, after killing an

Egyptian, Moses had to flee Egypt and so landed in a desert, caring for a flock that wasn't even his own. Nevertheless, it was to Moses in his midlife that God appeared. God chose Moses to set his people free. Ancient Israel's rescue from slavery in Egypt prefigured Jesus' death and resurrection, by which we are rescued from the slavery of sin. That's quite a mission Moses took up when it seemed that his life had been a failure.

If you wonder whether your time has passed, or whether you have ruined your opportunities, remember Moses. You too have a role to play in God's great plan of salvation.

Lord God, here I am.

29
The Lord Will Fight for You

Now Pharaoh was near when the Israelites looked up and saw that the Egyptians had set out after them. Moses answered the people, "Do not fear! Stand your ground and see the victory the LORD will win for you today. For these Egyptians whom you see today you will never see again. The LORD will fight for you; you have only to keep still."

Then the LORD said to Moses: Why are you crying out to me? Tell the Israelites to set out. And you, lift up your staff and stretch out your hand over the sea, and split it in two, that the Israelites may pass through the sea on dry land.

EXODUS 14:10, 13–16 (NABRE)

We live in a broken world where really bad things really do happen. When bad things happen, it is natural to feel that everything is beyond our control. There seems to be no way to save ourselves or provide for our loved ones. Think of the level of panic, the sleepless nights, the tears when there is not one dollar more to pay for groceries or rent or day care. The Israelites at the edge of the Red Sea were in just such a state of panic. They cried out in fear.

Even though they were anxious and afraid, God stood firm in his promise to free them. "The Lord will fight for you; you have only to keep still." And God did. When we are afraid, angry, and ready to blame someone for the predicament we are in, we can cry out to God, who will win the victory.

I am at peace, for your love is faithful.

30

An Immense Love

For I am about to create new heavens
    and a new earth;
the former things shall not be remembered
    or come to mind.
But be glad and rejoice forever
    in what I am creating;
for I am about to create Jerusalem as a joy,
    and its people as a delight.
I will rejoice in Jerusalem,
    and delight in my people;
no more shall the sound of weeping be heard in it,
    or the cry of distress.

Isaiah 65:17–19

In this passage, we are forced to stop and face the overwhelming, magnificent message of redemption: God is doing something new! It's not that God made a mistake at first. It's not that we had botched things up so badly that God decided to scrap everything and begin again with new people. Isaiah instead is painting a vision of love that has grown so immense it can create life, hope, and a future even in the midst of mistakes, sin, and death. This compassion is so divine that it straightens bent limbs, raises dead bodies and spirits, and transforms the dull and callous of heart. God will stop at nothing to make right our erring ways. He doesn't need to start over. Yesterday I saw a brave flower poking up through a crack in the sidewalk. The divine Lover is like this. Nothing can get in his way. He is unstoppable, for he has in mind to create something new of your life and mine.

Yes, Lord! Don't stop! Don't let me block your way! Do all that you desire to accomplish in my life!

Prayers

Psalm 23

The LORD is my shepherd, I shall not want.
    He makes me lie down in green pastures;
he leads me beside still waters;
    he restores my soul.
He leads me in right paths
    for his name's sake.
Even though I walk through the darkest valley,
    I fear no evil;
for you are with me;
    your rod and your staff—
    they comfort me.
You prepare a table before me
    in the presence of my enemies;
you anoint my head with oil;
    my cup overflows.
Surely goodness and mercy shall follow me
    all the days of my life,
and I shall dwell in the house of the LORD
    my whole life long.

Psalm 31

In you, O LORD, I seek refuge;
do not let me ever be put to shame;
in your righteousness deliver me.
Incline your ear to me;
rescue me speedily.
Be a rock of refuge for me,
a strong fortress to save me.
You are indeed my rock and my fortress;
for your name's sake lead me and guide me,
take me out of the net that is hidden for me,
for you are my refuge.
Into your hand I commit my spirit;
you have redeemed me, O LORD, faithful God.
You hate those who pay regard to worthless idols,
but I trust in the LORD.
I will exult and rejoice in your steadfast love,
because you have seen my affliction;
you have taken heed of my adversities,
and have not delivered me into the hand of the enemy;
you have set my feet in a broad place.
Be gracious to me, O LORD, for I am in distress;
my eye wastes away from grief,

my soul and body also.
For my life is spent with sorrow,
and my years with sighing;
my strength fails because of my misery,
and my bones waste away.
I am the scorn of all my adversaries,
a horror to my neighbors,
an object of dread to my acquaintances;
those who see me in the street flee from me.
I have passed out of mind like one who is dead;
I have become like a broken vessel.
For I hear the whispering of many—
terror all around!—
as they scheme together against me,
as they plot to take my life.
But I trust in you, O LORD;
I say, "You are my God."
My times are in your hand;
deliver me from the hand of my enemies and
persecutors.
Let your face shine upon your servant;
save me in your steadfast love.

Peace Prayer

Lord, make me an instrument of your peace.
Where there is hatred, let me sow love;
where there is injury, pardon;
where there is doubt, faith;
where there is despair, hope;
where there is darkness, light;
and where there is sadness, joy.
O Divine Master, grant that I may not so much
seek to be consoled as to console,
to be understood as to understand,
to be loved as to love.
For it is in giving that we receive,
it is in pardoning that we are pardoned,
and it is in dying that we are born to eternal life.

Saint Francis of Assisi

May God Give Us Peace

May God support us all the day long till the shades lengthen and the evening comes and the busy world is hushed and the fever of life is over and our work is done. Then in his mercy may God give us a safe lodging and a holy rest and peace at the last.

Saint John Henry Newman

In Times of Anxiety

Father, I know that your love never fails and that you care for everything you have made. Whatever the troubles of our hearts, you guide and sustain us. May the beauty of your creation—the lilies of the field and the birds of the air (see Luke 12:24, 27)—be a constant reminder to me that nothing you have made is ever forgotten.

In moments of fear, give me courage; when I am overwhelmed by anxiety, give me renewed faith in your loving Providence. I ask this through Jesus, your Son. Amen.

Mary Leonora Wilson, FSP

Help Me to Have Perfect Trust

O Christ Jesus, when all is darkness and I feel my weakness and helplessness, give me a sense of your presence, your love, and your strength. Help me to have perfect trust in your protecting love and strengthening power, so that nothing may frighten or worry me, for, living close to you, I shall see your hand, your purpose, your will through all things. Amen.

Saint Ignatius of Loyola

Prayer of Surrender

Father, I abandon myself into your hands;
do with me what you will.
Whatever you may do, I thank you;
I am ready for all, I accept all.
Let only your will be done in me,
and in all your creatures.
I wish no more than this, O Lord.
Into your hands I commend myself;
I offer myself to you with all the love of my heart,
for I love you, Lord, and so need to give myself,
to surrender myself into your hands without reserve,
and with boundless confidence, for you are my Father.

Saint Charles de Foucauld

Memorare

Remember, O most gracious Virgin Mary,
that never was it known
that anyone who fled to your protection,
implored your help, or sought your intercession
was left unaided.
Inspired with this confidence, I fly to you,

O Virgin of virgins, my Mother.
To you I come, before you I stand, sinful and
sorrowful.
O Mother of the Word Incarnate, despise not
my petitions,
but in your mercy hear and answer me. Amen.

Saint Bernard of Clairvaux

We Fly to Your Protection

We fly to your protection,
O holy Mother of God.
Despise not our petitions in our necessities,
but deliver us always from all dangers,
O glorious and blessed Virgin. Amen.

Oldest known prayer to the Virgin

For Those Awake This Night

O Lord, watch over those who are awake this night,
and give your angels and saints charge over those
who sleep.
Tend your sick ones, O Lord Christ.
Give rest to your weary ones,
bless your dying ones.
Provide comfort for your suffering ones

and compassion for your afflicted ones.
Protect your joyous ones.
All of this because you love us. Amen.

Saint Augustine

For Those Whom I Hold Dear

O my God! I ask you, for myself and for those whom I hold dear, the grace to fulfill perfectly your holy will, and to accept for love of you the joys and sorrows of this passing life, so that we may one day be united together in heaven for all eternity. Amen.

Saint Thérèse of Lisieux

That I May Not Worry . . .

Lord Jesus,
grant that I may not worry too much about
my life—what I will eat or what I will drink—
or about my body—what I will wear.
Help me to understand
that life is more than food,
and the body more than clothing.
Increase my faith in my heavenly Father,
who knows all my needs.

Increase my faith that by first seeking
God's kingdom and his will,
all these things will be given to me as well.

(see Matthew 6:25, 32–33)

Grant Me Peace . . .

Lord, grant me your peace, which is beyond all understanding,
and which will keep my heart and mind in Christ Jesus.
Fill my heart and my thoughts with all that is true,
honorable, just, pure, pleasing, gracious,
virtuous, and praiseworthy.
Grant me your peace, O Lord, and may it remain with me always.

(see Philippians 4:7–9)

Lord Jesus, Forsake Us Not

Lord Jesus, who was born for us in a stable, lived for us a life of pain and sorrow, and died for us upon a cross, say for us in the hour of death, "Father, forgive," and to your Mother, "Behold your child." Say to us, "This day you shall be with me in paradise." Dear Savior, leave us not, forsake us not. We thirst for you, Fountain of Living Water. Our days pass quickly; soon all will come to an end for us. Into your hands we commend our spirits, now and forever. Amen.

Saint Elizabeth Ann Seton

Pauline
BOOKS & MEDIA

A mission of the Daughters of St. Paul

As apostles of Jesus Christ,
evangelizing today's world:

We are CALLED to holiness
by God's living Word and Eucharist.

We COMMUNICATE the Gospel message
through our lives and through all
available forms of media.

We SERVE the Church
by responding to the hopes and needs
of all people with the Word of God,
in the spirit of St. Paul.

For more information visit us at:
www.pauline.org